THIS BOOK IS

....

THE WORLD'S MOST HORRIFIC/
GORGEOUS/SMELLY/REVOLTING/
LOVABLE/VILE/SMASHING/ARIEN

WITH LOTS OF LOVE/ DROP DEAD/
BEST WISHES FROM ....

P.S. PLEASE TAKE NOTE OF PAGE(S)

....

THE ARIES BOOK

A CORGI BOOK 0 552 12316 1

First publication in Great Britain
PRINTING HISTORY
Corgi edition published 1983
Corgi edition reissued 1984

Corgi Books are published by Transworld Publishers Ltd.,
Century House, 61-63 Uxbridge Road, Ealing, London W5 5SA.

Made and printed in Great Britain by the
Guernsey Press Co. Ltd., Guernsey, Channel Islands.

THE ARIES BOOK

BY

IAN HEATH

ARIES

MARCH 21 – APRIL 20

FIRST SIGN OF THE ZODIAC
SYMBOL: THE RAM
RULING PLANET: MARS
COLOURS: VERMILION, MUSTARD
GEMS: RUBY, BLOODSTONE
NUMBER: NINE
DAY: TUESDAY
METAL: IRON
FLOWER: ANEMONE

.... IS PERSUASIVE..................

..... LIKES A CHALLENGE.........

..........IS FRIENDLY..............

...... TAKES SHORT CUTS............

.....LIKES TO START AT THE TOP........

.... DISLIKES REGULAR HOURS........

.... MAKES QUICK DECISIONS..........

.... KEEPS COOL IN A CRISIS.........

.... IS LEVEL-HEADED..............

.......AND IS CUNNING.

The
ARIEN
finds success as......

.... A SURGEON..............

.... MECHANIC...............

...... CHICKEN-PLUCKER...........

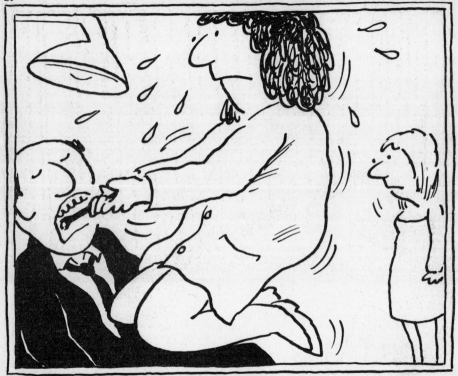

.... DENTIST..................

.... LUMBERJACK...............

.... GLASSBLOWER ....

..... OR DEEP-SEA FISHERMAN.

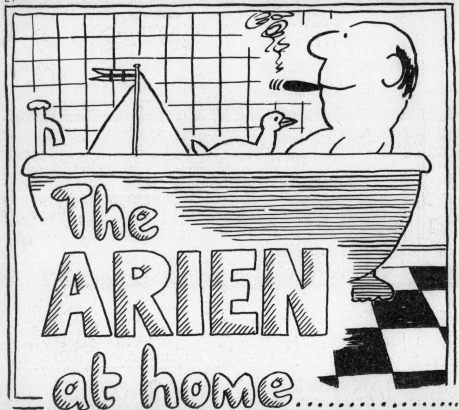

The ARIEN at home.................

...... HAS REGULAR CLEAR-OUTS.......

.............IS A GOSSIP...................

.... A BIT CARELESS...............

......NEEDS GENTLE HANDLING......

.....TAKES REGULAR EXERCISE.........

.......KEEPS UNUSUAL PETS............

.......RULES THE ROOST.............

..... HAS FEW POSSESSIONS.........

...SPENDS A LOT ON FOOD............

.... AND LOVES CHILDREN.

The
ARIEN
likes.........................

.... SPAGHETTI ....

..........ICE – SKATING...............

....BEING WHERE THE ACTION IS........

..........CANDY-FLOSS...............

.... BIRD-WATCHING ....

.... AND SPORT ON TELLY.

The
ARIEN
dislikes.............

.... BEING PHOTOGRAPHED........

... HAVING THEIR HAIR DONE...........

.... SMELLY FEET ....

46

..........NOSE-PICKERS..............

.... AUTHORITY...................

RING!
RING!

RING! RI......

.... AND TELEPHONES.

The
ARIEN
in love..................

.......TAKES THE INITIATIVE...........

.... IS DIRECT...................

.... LIKES FLATTERY..............

......HAS A ROVING EYE............

54

...... ALWAYS ON THE 'PHONE ....

.....LIKES BEING HUGGED..........

.... ENJOYS ROMANTIC PLACES ....

.........BEING TICKLED.................

.....AND......

ARIEN
AND PARTNER

HEART RATINGS

♥♥♥♥♥ WOWEE.!!
♥♥♥♥ GREAT, BUT NOT 'IT'
♥♥♥ O.K. — COULD BE FUN
♥♥ FORGET IT
♥ WALK QUICKLY THE OTHER WAY

LEO   SAGITTARIUS

TAURUS GEMINI PISCES
AQUARIUS

CANCER LIBRA ARIES

CAPRICORN

VIRGO SCORPIO

ARIES PEOPLE

HANS CHRISTIAN ANDERSEN
GREGORY PECK : ROD STEIGER
HARRY HOUDINI : CASANOVA
JOAN CRAWFORD : DORIS DAY
ALEC GUINNESS : HENRY JAMES

WILBUR WRIGHT : BISMARCK
BESSIE SMITH : OMAR SHARIF
MARLON BRANDO : BETTE DAVIS
PAUL ROBESON : STEVE McQUEEN
TENNESSEE WILLIAMS
CHARLES CHAPLIN : F.W. WOOLWORTH
PETER USTINOV : DEBBIE REYNOLDS
VINCENT VAN GOGH
BILLIE HOLIDAY : KRUSHCHEV
SPENCER TRACY : PEARL BAILEY
ARTURO TOSCANINI